Best green Home projects

Brenda K. Cross

Spirit Hills
PUBLISHING

*"The only way to implement our vision for society
is to bring it down to the situation of a single household."*
Chogyam Trungpa Rinpoche

20/20 Enterprises, Inc.
presents

Best Green Home Projects:
25 Weatherization Projects for a Greener Home and Business

Brenda K. Cross

A Spirit Hills Book

ISBNO 0-9763322-2-1

Third Edition

Book Design: Imagination To Go!
www.ImaginationToGo.com

Printed in the United States of America
on recycled paper (30%+ post-consumer waste)

Hi, People!

This book is NOT for everyone. This book is for DOERS! It's easy to sit around and complain about high utility bills, but complaining will not lower them. DOING these projects WILL LOWER your utility bills and $ave Your Green. It's your money, you know!

Most of these simple projects cost less than $100. Many can be done in under an hour. You will $ave money and improve the comfort level in your home. Now THAT is what I call **$aving Your Green!**

Imagine telling someone looking to buy or rent your home, ***"Your utility bills will be 10%-30% lower than your neighbors! This means, you will save about $___ + each year."*** What a great selling point!

Does it work? I live in Austin, Texas. It is HOT! Like 90+ degrees about six months per year and unfiltered sun! My condo was 30 years old; the HVAC system and water heater were 12 years old. Floor to ceiling windows facing south and west! HOT!

My neighbor's utility bills averaged $190-$345/mo. After completing these projects, my bills averaged $125/mo. My home is a comfortable 76° in the summer and 70° in the winter. ***DOING*** these "projects" has made the difference in my utility bills and it can do the same thing for you.

Different companies, organizations and agencies have recommended many of these projects, in various formats, for years. Others, I created by experimenting on my home. All have proven effective in making my home more comfortable. I have just put them all in one easy to use book ... for everyone.

"But, I don't know how to make improvements" ... oh, please! Do you want some cheese with that whine? I am a single, "middle-aged" woman of average size and like you, busier than heck. If I can do it, you can too!

Now, let's DO and have some FUN!

Most of the projects I did myself or recruited friends and neighbors to assist with trickier or heavier projects, like ceiling fans, programmable thermostat, etc. Most folks are willing to help out, and working together creates community. Just ask.

Several brand names are mentioned. I am not trying to advertise for them; I'm just telling you what I used. There are many brands of everything, use what works best, shop where you prefer; this is your home, even if you rent!

My mom always told me, "Just do your best and that will be good enough." I have done that with this manual. I leave you with her same good advice, "just do your best . . ."!

First, a bit of required legal stuff: There are no warranties or guarantees implied or otherwise. The author, publisher, distributors and/or seller's of this book are not liable in any way for any activities undertaken in this book or the results to either your home and/or your physical being. Follow factory instructions and safety directions on all products—things change!

ABOVE ALL, BE SAFE!

Wear Safety Glasses Especially when what you're working on is overhead, is chemical, or spits.

Wear Disposable Gloves when working with finger stuff.

Use Height-Appropriate Step Stools and Ladders

Take Your Time! This isn't a race, it's a process! It took me awhile to finish! The $aving$ are worth it!

Read Directions ALWAYS follow factory directions & safety instructions; things change!

HAVE FUN! Put on your favorite tunes. Involve family, friends or neighbors!

Laugh Having more money for things other than utility bills . . . is FUN . . . and PRODUCTIVE!

(Check off what you have now – then tear this sheet out and take it as a shopping list!)

Claw Hammer: *(Your choice of style & cost)*	$ 5–$15	☐
2–Step Step Stool	$10–$20	☐
2–Phillips Head Screwdrivers		
(1 with a "fat" head, 1 with "slim" head)	$1–$2 ea.	☐
2–Flat Head Screwdrivers	$1–$2 ea.	☐
Caulk Gun	$4–$6	☐
Package of Disposable Gloves	$2–$3	☐
Pointed Shovel	$10–$15	☐
25' Tape Measure	$3–$5	☐
Nail Set	$1–$3	☐
Lightweight Spackle (Smallest size)	$3–$4	☐
5' to 6' Step Ladder	$20–$35	☐
Small Miter Box	$12–$30	☐
Inexpensive Safety Glasses	$2–$4	☐
Utility/Razor Knife	$3–$5	☐

> *Really GREEN TIP:*
> *Borrow and/or share*
> *what you need for or*
> *already have BEFORE*
> *you buy new! Start*
> *a "Community Tool*
> *Sharing" program.*

Total Investment: $77–$149

Household Items

Paper Towels

9 Volt Batteries (5 or 6)

Scissors

Flashlight (that works)

Old Sponges & Rags – worn clothing

Large Nail or Screw

Ruler

Pencil

Isopropyl Alcohol

Non-Toxic Glass Cleaner

STAPLE YOUR RECEIPTS HERE!

 >>

Why reduce air flow into and out of your home? Well, open your door and step outside — go ahead, do it! Is it too hot? Too cold? Too humid?

Plugging air leaks in your home means greater physical comfort year-round AND lower heating and cooling bills, even if you keep your thermostat set the same as you do now. Make a few adjustments, and they can drop further!

Not only will your bills decline, your home will have fewer 'hot' and 'cold' spots; especially if you use window coverings in a common sense manner. It may even reduce the number of insects that manage to find their way in … after all, if air can come through it — more than likely a bug can too!

As detailed on the "Disclaimers" page; after doing these projects, my electric and water bills dropped; compared to what my neighbors told me theirs were … mine were 25%-50% lower. These projects PAY YOU BACK! And who can put a price tag on comfort? Want some "extra" $pending money? This is the place to start!

A question often asked: "Doesn't a house have to breathe?" Well, yes; and if your house is 10+ years old, it is almost impossible (by doing these projects) to prevent it from breathing! Many larger and energy efficient homes have Air Exchangers that provide that function. Personally, I have never been able to seal a home so completely that it did not breathe! ☺

Tear out this list and save it for future trips, if you choose to buy these items on an "as needed" basis. Does NOT include products from General Shopping List.

Leak Proof Your Outlets – Project

1 or 2 packs each foam outlet insulators @ $2/pack
Count light switches and wall outlets: _____

Caulk It! Inside Windows – Project

Interior Paintable Caulk 25+ years.
1 Tube Caulk = 3 Large to 6 Small Windows (approx)
Count Windows _____ x $4–$5/tube   _____

Caulk It! Outside Windows – Project

Outdoor Caulk ~ 25+ years
1 Tube Caulk = 3 Large to 6 Small Windows (approx)
Count Windows _____ x $5–$7/tube   _____

Plexi-It! Your Non-Opening Windows – Project

Measure ALL windows you wish to cover:
Length ____ x Width ____
Length ____ x Width ____
Length ____ x Width ____
Length ____ x Width ____
Plexiglas® cut to the size of your windows–$8 to $25.
Hint: Windows 36" or less, use thinner plexi. Over 36" use
¼" Plexi or thicker. Color is up to you.
#Windows? _____
Indoor Caulk @ $4–$5/tube   _____
Optional: 1 Can Great Stuff® for Windows/Doors   _____
Quarter-Round Wood Trim @ $.35 -$.50/ft.   _____
    Length x 2 + Width x 2 = Total Trim for 1 Window
2" Inexpensive Paint Brush @ $3–$4   _____
1 lb. of 1½" Finishing Nails @ $2–$3   _____
Paint for trim to complement your home   _____

Strip It! Your Outside Doors – Project

Metal Weather Stripping Door Kit (3 pieces) @ $15–$20

Door Sweeps for inside home – about $8–$20 each

Count # Doors that need it _____

Strip It! Basement and/or Attic Doors – Project

Door Sweeps for bottom of doors @ $8–$20 _____

Half- Moon Shaped Puffy Weather Stripping on a

Roll w/Adhesive Back @ $5–$7 _____

Foiling Your Duct Leaks – Project

1 – 2 rolls FOIL TAPE @ $6–$8/roll _____

OR 1 Can Mastic @ $15/can _____

Flue-Plugs! – Project

BEST Option: Purchase & install glass fireplace doors

OR ¾"-1" Wide Double Stick Tape @ $3-$5 _____

OR ¾"-1" Wide Velcro™ @ $5-$9 _____

Plexiglas® – Cut size of fireplace opening @ $35 _____

Important note: Depending on where you live, you may be eligible for state or local tax deductions and/or rebates ... or this may benefit you with your corporate sponsored program!

**STAPLE YOUR RECEIPTS HERE
ON THIS PAGE!** >>

Tools/Supplies Needed:

1 Small Flat Head Screwdriver

1 or 2 packs each foam outlet insulators

(some for light switches and others for wall outlets)

Approximate Time:

One Hour – total

Now What?

1. Start in the kitchen of your home and work your way around the all the walls that face the **outside** (interior walls, generally don't need insulating – see #5 below).
2. Turn off power at junction box or breaker box (one room at a time is usually best).
3. Remove face plates from electrical outlets & light switches with screwdrivers. This is also a great time to clean the face plates.
4. Remove perforated outlet sections on the foam. Slide the insulator over outlets/light switches until snug against wall.
5. Replace face plate & screw(s).
6. If you have a 2nd floor on your home, repeat this process until ALL outlets on ALL outside walls are insulated. (If your home is pier-and-beam, you should also do interior wall outlets.)

Optional Activity

While you have the face plate off, visually inspect the outlet. Look at (don't touch) the wires. Do they look worn or frayed? If so, consider calling an electrician.

If your face plates are cracked, consider new ones: the standard plastic variety cost $.25 to $.50 each and come in white or cream. OR if they are just ugly, paint the old ones to match your walls. ☺

Remove Outlet Covers — Plugs and Light Switches

Remove perforated
cut-outs from foam
insulators (outlet is shown,
but switches work the
same way).

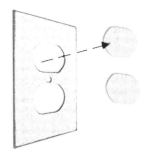

Place insulator over outlet. Replace cover.

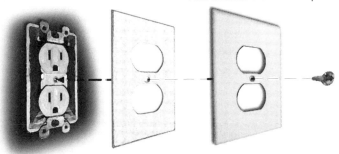

*Note: Most insulators are designed for single electrical boxes, but you can customize two or more
of them to fit under double or triple electrical box covers. Overlap three insulators to provide a
tight seal under a triple cover plate, rather than trimming to size.*

Tools/Supplies Needed:
Caulk Gun and Inside Caulk from your Shopping List
Paper Towels — Glass Cleaner—Plastic Gloves (if desired)
Ladder or Step Stool if necessary

Approximate Time:
30-50 Minutes per window

Now What?
1. Remove window coverings and CLEAN window with non-toxic glass cleaner. Remove fingerprints and dust. Let window dry.
2. Inspect for cracks and spaces between the window frame and wall, and under the window sill between the sill and trim piece, etc.
3. Put the tube of caulk into gun. Squeeze trigger to tighten until screw portion touches the bottom of tube.
4. Snip end of caulk tube at an ANGLE making a ¼" opening.
5. Grasp trigger and gently squeeze, starting at any corner where frame of window meets wall. Run a line of caulk to the next corner, until you have finished the window.
6. Fill all cracks with caulk: corners, under window sill and between the sill and trim piece.
7. Whenever you set the caulk gun down, loosen the pressure by depressing the lever and pulling the pin back ... otherwise, caulk will continue to seep out.
8. Get a cup of water, paper towels and plastic gloves (if you prefer). Wet finger; smooth caulk lines, one side at a time, so cracks are sealed. Wipe excess caulk on paper towels. IMPORTANT: Keep you finger wet and clean as you go. Caulk will stick to your finger; it WON'T stick to water.
9. Repeat the process on each window until all are done.
10. Let dry 24 hours before painting.

Gently replace window coverings. Avoid bumping the caulk. Easy huh?

Remember to inspect window caulk every year!

Inside and/or Outside!
Remove Window Coverings
and Clean Glass

Load Caulk Gun

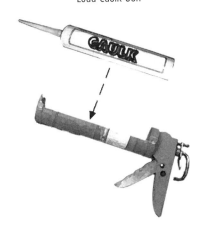

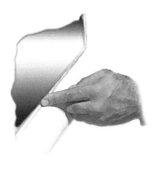

Start Here where window
frame meets window casing

Smooth Caulk w/Finger

Tools/Supplies Needed:

Caulk Gun and Inside Caulk from your Shopping List
Paper Towels — Glass Cleaner — Plastic Gloves (if desired)
Ladder to reach windows — as high as it makes sense

Time Needed:

40-50 Minutes per window

Now What?

1. CLEAN window with non-toxic glass cleaner. Remove fingerprints and dust. Make sure everything is totally dry.
2. Inspect for cracks and spaces between the window frame and wall and/or exterior window trim.
3. Put the tube of caulk into gun. Squeeze trigger to tighten until screw portion touches the bottom of tube.
4. Snip end of caulk tube at an ANGLE making a ¼" opening.
5. Grasp trigger and gently squeeze, starting at any corner where frame of window meets wall. Run a line of caulk to the next corner, until you have finished the window.
6. Fill all cracks with caulk: corners, under window sill and between the sill and trim piece.
7. Whenever you set the caulk gun down, loosen the pressure by depressing the lever and pulling the pin back ... otherwise, caulk will continue to seep out.
8. Get a cup of water, paper towels and plastic gloves (if you prefer). Wet finger; smooth caulk lines, one side at a time, so cracks are sealed. Wipe excess caulk on paper towels. IMPORTANT: Keep you finger wet and clean as you go. Caulk will stick to your finger; it WON'T stick to water.
9. Repeat the process on each window until all are done.
10. Let dry 24 hours before painting.

HINT: BIG GAPS — LOTS OF AIR?

Follow directions on "Great Stuff™ for Doors and Windows". This is EXPANDO FOAM: A LITTLE BIT gets a LOT BIGGER! Let cure for about 3 hours. Remove over-expansion with a knife then paint over the yellow stuff! *WEAR SAFETY GLASSES!*

Tools/Supplies Needed:

Ladder ~ tall enough to reach desired windows

Acrylic Glass ~ cut to size of windows (from $12 to $75)

Glass Cleaner	Paper Towels	Pencil & Paper
Soapy Water/Cloth		Measuring Tape
Plastic Knife	Nail Set	Quarter-Round Trim

1 can Great Stuff for Windows & Doors™ – Optional

Small Miter Box, Claw Hammer, Paint Brush, Finishing Nails, Caulk Gun, Safety Glasses, Spackle and Indoor 25-year Paintable Caulk as per shopping lists.

Paint for Quarter Round Trim to compliment your home

Hint: Use "Low or NO VOC" paint to help eliminate the chemical paint smells that off-gas into your home; these can cause headaches and other physical ailments, especially important if you have allergies or chemical sensitivities.

Now What?

1. Remove ANY window coverings AND brackets!
2. CLEAN window, edges and glass with non-toxic Glass Cleaner
3. Clean the sill and frame around window with soapy water. Remove all dirt and debris!

Phase One ~ Time Needed: 45–60 minutes per window

REPEAT all the Steps for Caulking your Windows, found in the CAULK-IT chapter of this book (if not already done). Let caulk "cure" over night.

*HINT: Fill in Large gaps between the window frame and sill, with "Great Stuff™". Let cure over night. Remove over expansion with sharp knife the next day. **WEAR SAFETY GLASSES!***

Phase Two ~ Time Needed: 1 to 2 hours

1. Paint all your trim. Let paint dry.
2. Paint with 2nd coat. Let paint dry.

continued ...

Phase Three ~ Time Needed: 30 minutes per window – *(Do this while first coat of paint is drying up there in Phase 1)*
1. Peel off protective coating from back of glass.
2. Fit glass snugly against the edge of window frame.(It will ½" to 1" away from window, providing an air barrier).
3. Place a small tack or nail in the center of the window frame wall on each side to hold glass in place (temporary installment).

Phase Four ~ Time Needed: 45 minutes per window
1. Measure all sides of the windows you intend to cover.
   a) Top _____ Left _____ Bottom _____ Right _____
   b) Top _____ Left _____ Bottom _____ Right _____
   c) Top _____ Left _____ Bottom _____ Right _____
   d) Top _____ Left _____ Bottom _____ Right _____
   e) Top _____ Left _____ Bottom _____ Right _____
2. Mark window measurements above, off onto Quarter Round Trim. Miter Trim ends to fit together. (see following page). Miter box will have this angle notated in both directions.
3. Cut all for pieces for the Window A above.
4. Remove one supporting nail from one side of glass and begin.
5. Peel all protective film off the glass.
6. Snug flat trim side against the glass-the other is against the wall.
7. Using Finishing Nails, nail trim into wall. Complete all sides of window in this manner.
8. Inset nails by placing point of Nail Set onto head of nail. Tap gently with hammer until nail is recessed into trim.
9. Spackle holes over top of nails. Touch up paint if desired.
10. Repeat until all windows are completed. *(This process will be easier on the next window – I promise ☺).*

NOTE: *This project reduced my heat upstairs significantly! I had five 35" x 35" single pane windows, letting in a lot of hot sun and leaking air. My upstairs became far more comfortable after finishing this one and my energy bills went down even more.*

Non-Opening Window ~ Clean and Caulk Edges

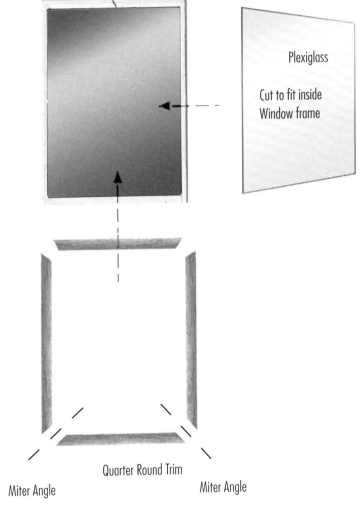

Plexiglass

Cut to fit inside
Window frame

Quarter Round Trim

Miter Angle

Miter Angle

Miter as indicated

FIRST: *Check each door for weather stripping. REPLACE it only if you can see light around the edges of your doors OR you can feel a breeze coming in around the edges! Unless your doors are overly large, the standard kit will fit!*

Tools/Supplies Needed:

3 – Piece Metal Weather Stripping Door Kit
Door Sweeps – IF there is LIGHT coming in UNDER doors!
Claw Hammer   Cloth   Screw Driver (maybe)

Time Needed:

45-60 minutes per door

Now What?

1. Take hammer and remove old weather stripping. Trash it. Scrape off any accumulated "gunk" and clean thoroughly.
2. Slide top of door weather stripping in place on outside of door frame, until the "puffy P" part is snuggled (NOT Mashed!) up against the outside top of your door.
3. Nail in place in the holes provided with nails provided.
4. Slide long side pieces of weather stripping into place on each side of door and nail in place in the holes provided.

Door Sweep: *If you see light under the bottom of your door, install a door sweep.*

Time Needed:

45-60 minutes per door

Now What?

1. Line up Sweep so it barely clears floor covering.
2. Fasten with 1" nails or screws (provided) on each end
3. Affix balance of nails or screws into the sweep in holes provided.

No more door drafts ☺

Remove old weather
stripping next to door

Install new weather stripping with
"Puffy" P Side next to door; Tack
to top and both sides of door frame.

Add a Door Sweep
to control drafts

Attic? Basement? WHY? Check it out: your attic and basement are never the same temperature as the rest of your house. Insulation reduces airflow when the doors are closed, especially at the bottom of the door … and that makes for more efficient heat and air.

FIRST: Is there light around the door edges or bottom? If not, SKIP this section. If so, then purchase the same door sweeps and weather stripping kits as you did for your outside doors!

Tools/Supplies Needed:
> 3-Piece Door Weather Stripping Kit
> Door Sweeps
> ATTIC: Puffy Half-Moon Shaped Stripping w/Adhesive Back
> Claw Hammer
> Screwdriver (maybe)

Time Needed:
> 30-45 minutes per door

Now What?
1. Place Door Sweep at bottom of door on side opening OUT and tack into place. Sweep should block out light, but the door still should open easily.
2. Place Side/Top Weather Stripping on opposite side of door as door sweep. Install the same as outside doors.
3. Pull Down Attic Door and extend staircase. Clean around edge of door framing.
4. Cut correct lengths of Half-moon stripping to fit all sides of door frame.
5. Peel backing from adhesive side about 12" and begin sticking the stripping about ¼" above bottom of frame.
6. Continue until all sides are stripped.
7. Fold up staircase and close door.

That's It Folks !

for Door Sweeps & Attic Stripping

Pull-Down Attic Storage
strip around edges.

Add fiberglass insulation between
steps for even more savings.

Door Sweeps: Basement, Garage,
Attic — any exterior door. They are easy
to install and increase energy efficiency.

FIRST: Turn on AIR. Then check all exposed HVAC ducts. Go into the attic, above your ceilings, into your basement and/or under your house in the crawl space. *FEEL* where your ducts are connected for air coming out of them! Mark LEAKS with Red Marker or Sharpie. Sealing these leaks can cut your energy bill by as much as 15%-35%.

Tools/Supplies Needed:
1-2 Rolls Foil Tape
Scissors
Soapy Water or Spray Cleaner & Cleaning Cloth
Red Magic Marker
Optional: Mastic

Time Needed:
10-30 minutes per leak

Now What?
1. CLEAN separated connections areas and let them dry.
2. Cut two 6"-12" length of FOIL Tape. Reconnect ducts and secure with tape strips.
3. WRAP foil tape around the entire seam 3 times around. First around seam ... Next super seal one side then super seal the other. STOP the air from leaking!
4. Repeat with all other leak areas until completed.
5. TURN ON the air again. Go back and double check all marked connections to make sure all leaks are totally sealed.

OPTIONAL: Mastic. Mastic is an excellent sealer for METAL (not flexible) duct work. FOLLOW FACTORY INSTRUCTIONS for application.

I prefer foil tape. It is easier and more economical. You will need to CHECK for leaks at least every 1-2 years ... or if you see an unexpected spike in your utility bill. If your ductwork is in the walls and cannot be inspected, hire an HVAC duct cleaning/ inspection company.

Note: My mother's electric use dropped 550 KWH/month once her ducts were fixed – a $60/month SAVINGS on her bill! By the way, she did the work herself ... and she is over 70!

No, this is NOT a new disease — just easy ways to end the air flow up/from your chimney! Let's start with the obvious: If you have glass doors on your fireplace, close the flue ~ close & lock the doors! Done! Nothing more needed!

If you don't have airtight doors, you can purchase & install them for $75–$250. Want to spend less? Try this:

Tools/Supplies Needed:

Cleaning Cloth   Safety Glasses
Flashlight   Isopropyl Alcohol
¾"-1" Wide Double Stick Tape   OR   ¾"-1" Wide Roll Velcro™
Acrylic Glass — Cut to size of fireplace opening (I used Plexi)

Time Needed:

45 Minutes or so

Now What?

1. Put on Safety Glasses and clean fireplace. Use the flashlight to make sure flue is closed.
2. With alcohol, clean all the way around the OUTSIDE of the metal "insert" framing your firebox. No insert? Clean from outer edge of firebox inside about 3". Let dry.
3. Cut twelve 3" long strips of Velcro™ or double-stick tape. You may need more if your firebox is especially large.
4. *With insert:* Peel off one side of tape or backing from Velcro™. Stick in four corners then space two each across top and bottom; space one between corners on each side.
   No Insert: Have glass cut 1" larger than firebox and Velcro™ or double-stick tape to OUTSIDE of firebox as per above instructions. Velcro™ is recommended.
5. Remove protective covering from both sides of glass.
6. Slide glass into place. Peel off tape backing or add the other side of the Velcro™ affixed to the glass, to match fireplace application.
7. Push glass into place, letting tape on edges grab the back of the glass. Slow and steady insures a snug seal.

NOTE: If you have a wood edge around firebox, cut glass 2" larger than opening. Use thin ¾" screws to screw through glass into the wood completely covering opening.

Tear out this list and save it for future trips, if you choose to buy these items on an "as needed" basis. Does NOT include products from General Shopping List .

Plant It! $hading Your Home *Project*

50-100 lbs. good potting soil @ $10–$20 _____

1 Small Tree that grows well in your area with little
maintenance or water. @ $30–$70 _____

Wheelbarrow or cart — borrow one or spend $20+ _____

Pointed Digging Shovel from Master Shopping List

Solar Screens OR Shade Cloth OR Window Film *Project*

FIRST: Measure ALL windows to be covered:

Length _____ x Width _____ Lgth _____ x Width _____

Length _____ x Width _____ Lgth _____ x Width _____

Start with those having exposure to west, south and southwest

Shade Cloth and/or Window Film $10–$50/window _____

Film Adhesive Applicator @ $5 _____

Squeegee Kit @ $5 _____

(Research and call 3 Solar Screen Companies for Bids)

Shading Your HVAC Unit *Project*

4 - 8' tall metal notched fence posts @ $5 - $9 ea _____

3 - 4'x8' Sheets of Lattice preferably non-wood _____

3 - Shrubs native to your part of the country that
grow at least 4' tall _____

1 Package Wire Tie Wraps 8"-12" long @ $5-$7 _____

Electric Water Heater – Insulate It! *Project*

"Space Age"™ or thermal Water Tank Insulation Blanket @ $20 _____

Slit Foam Tape Insulation for Pipes @ $3–$6 _____

Staple Receipts Here!

Trees will never be beat for natural shading. ☺ According to many studies, a well placed tree that shades the hottest part of your house can reduce utility bills by 15 - 35%. I LOVE my trees … they cool my home all summer long!

Tools/Supplies Needed:

Pointed Shovel

50–100 lbs. of good potting soil

Tree that grows well in your area without a lot of maintenance or 'extra' water.

Borrowed wheelbarrow, wagon or cart

Time Needed:

3 Hours

Now What?

1. Choose the hottest spot closest to unprotected windows.
2. Pace off about 25' from that spot. Remember, trees grow to be large! We want is shade – not foundation roots!
3. Dig a hole 2-3 times larger than tree's root ball.
4. Pour 8" – 12" of good dirt in the bottom of the hole.
5. Get help (if needed) to move the tree (wheelbarrow).
6. Cut the sack off the root ball UNLESS it is biodegradable and there is NO wire binding.
7. Plant tree so root ball is below ground according to tree planting instructions
8. Fill in around tree with removed and new dirt. Periodically stomp/tamp dirt down to insure tree is well planted.
9. When tree is planted – water thoroughly.
10. Follow the instructions for watering and care to keep your young tree healthy and growing. Enjoy the natural shade and greater comfort in your home that is will provide!

Solar Screens OR Shade Cloth OR Window Film

SHADE CLOTH or WINDOW FILM: If solar screens are just not an option, consider Shade Cloth or Window Film. Benefits: Dramatically reduced summer heat keeps home cooler; Lower electric bill; Less Furniture Fading!

SOLAR Screens & Where to Find Them: Yellow Pages under Solar Screens. *Or ask your neighbors who have Solar Screen. Or a trusted retail person. About 1 hour on the phone. (This option is my personal preference).*

Information Needed: Window Sizes per shopping list. This is an OUTSIDE the house job, you won't need to be there. *In my experience, Solar Screens are NOT expensive.* Get 3 Bids.
NOTE: Remove solar screens in the winter by unscrewing them from window frame. This allows heat and sun into your home during colder months. Re-install when it gets hot again.

Tools/Supplies Needed:
>   Enough shade cloth or window film to block sunny windows.
>   Use your measurements!
>   Shade Cloth – Choice of colors. $55–$75 per roll   _____
>   Window Film – Choice of shades. $20-$25/roll   _____
>   Window Film Application Spray @ $6-$7   _____
>   Squeegee/Knife Kit @ $5   _____

Approximate Time:
>   45 minutes to 1 hour per window.

Now What?
1. **For Shade Cloth:** cut the "cloth" to the length of window
2. Install on the outside or inside of windows; by using small, stainless nails to secure shade cloth.
3. Remove cloth in the winter to allow sun/heat into home.
1. **For Solar Film:** follow factory instructions! Clean windows!
2. Apply per directions and take it slowly!

I prefer FILM to Shade Cloth: it looks better and allows for excellent visibility out your window!

FIRST: Go outside and LOOK at the location of your HVAC unit. Is it shaded by trees or your house most of the day? If so – than this project isn't necessary. If NOT…continue on …

Tools/Supplies Needed:

4 - 8' tall metal notched fence posts
Sledge Hammer
3 – 4' x 8' Sheets of Lattice preferably non-wood
Pointed Shovel
3 Native Shrubs that will grow to at least 4' tall
Wire Tie Wraps – 8"-12" long

Approximate Time:

2-4 Hours

Now What?

1. Measure at least 18" from sides of unit and dig 4 small holes for stakes, at least 6"-12" deep or sledge hammer the stakes into the ground to the same depth.
2. Plant stakes and backfill with dirt *(optional: concrete)* for security. Tamp well.
3. Cut lattice to correct height of stakes. The side closest to the house will not be latticed.
4. Secure corners of lattice with tie wraps to the stakes. Secure the top first and then the bottom, squaring up the edges. Tie wrap lattice to metal poles every 12"-18" Lattice permits free flow of HOT air away from the unit and prevents over-heating.
5. Once the lattice is secured, plant the shrubs. Dig a hole for each shrub outside and center of each latticed side. Hole should be 6" larger in diameter and 3" deeper than shrubs root ball.
6. Plant shrubs. Backfill holes with dirt and water them well. In 2-3 years they will be big enough to shade your HVAC unit without the lattice. Trimming occasionally will keep them healthy and attractive.

The goal is to shade your unit without anything touching it, getting 'sucked in' by it or getting caught in it! An HVAC unit can literally burn up without fresh air circulating freely!

Keeping the "hot" inside your water heater is only smart!

Tools/Supplies Needed:
> "Space Age"™ or Thermal Water Tank Insulation Blanket @ $20
> Self Seal Foam Pipe Insulation
> Scissors or Utility Knife
> Step Stool
> Measuring Tape

RECOMMENDED:
> Water Heater Programmable TIMER ($40–$50). Installation requires a
> plumber and an electrician, but adding a timer can reduce electric bills by $20-$40
> per month!

Time Needed:
> 30-45 minutes

Now What?
1. Measure each pipe and cut pipe insulation to the correct length with utility knife. Slip over pipe. Seal with tape (attached).
2. Wrap insulation blanket around your tank and tape it per instructions, with enclosed tape. You might need to trim it if it is a bit too long, with scissors.
3. Measure across the TOP of your tank – write down: ___
4. Use left over insulation and cut 2 pieces to that length.
5. Place on top of tank. Cut out for pipes, valves, etc.; trim up the sides so it is round.
6. Tape firmly in place engaging the top of the tank insulation.
7. Tape bottom edge of insulation to tank. DONE!

FREEBIE: Lower temperature on tank to 120º This will reduce your energy bill and reduce the chances of someone getting burned by hot water. Not to worry, your dishwasher has a heating element and hot water NEVER is connected to your dishwasher!

There are many simple technological products that assist with saving energy. Of course, in keeping with this book, they are simple to understand and generally less than $100. So let's start shopping!

Shopping List For Better Technology

Total of 4 Projects … tear out this list. Save for future trips, if you choose to buy these items on an "as needed" basis.

Light Up Your Life! Indoors *Project*

8-10 Compact Fluorescent light bulbs (to start)
Standard Lights for closets, porch lights, laundry room, garage, basements. $10/4-pack   _____
Bright whites for all else — bath, rooms, fans, etc.
"Day-Lighting" bulbs for Reading/Desk Lamps   _____

Light Up the Night *Project*

Solar Powered motion sensor floodlights
@ $60–$90   _____
Solar Powered Accent/Path Lights
@ $70 to $300   _____

Program It! ~ Techno "Brain" *Project*

Programmable Thermostat @ $40 -$110   _____
(NOTE: The more features, the more expensive this one gets. If you have a heat pump, this will run at least $100.

Shut It ALL Off ~ Zip Strips *Project*

1-3 Multiple-outlet Power Strips @ $12 to $50 ea   _____
1-3 "Light" Timers (optional) @ $5–$7 ea   _____

STAPLE RECEIPTS HERE

Tools/Supplies Needed:

Step Stool or Short Ladder
8 to 10 Compact Fluorescent Light Bulbs (to start)
Buy different sizes and light colors to fit your fixtures & uses
Maybe a small Flat-head Screwdriver

Approximate Time:

30 – 45 minutes max

Now What?

1. 1. WRITE with your sharpie marker on the BASE of your bulb, the date of installation and the initial of the store where you bought it. (Ex: 1-21-11/L) If it burns out 'early', you know where to ask for a refund! (Helpful hint courtesy of Harry Grossman.)
2. Start with your porch lights, garage, basement, closet & laundry lights. Remove light covering (use screwdriver if necessary.) Unscrew bulb. Grasp CFL by the BASE—not the 'curly' part of the bulb—to avoid breaking. Carefully screw in CFL bulb.
3. Repeat process with all other bulbs. Should last at least 5 years.

At the end of 30 minutes, you should have replaced at least 10 lights with CFL's (compact fluorescents). You can replace them all at one time or as your budget allows.

Hints:

- Buy 2 or 3 CFL bulbs every month. As your standard bulbs burn out, replace them with fluorescents. By year's end you won't have to worry about changing bulbs.
- Garage-door opener lights and ceiling fans require special vibration-resistant bulbs. You may need to hunt a bit to find these special CFL bulbs.
- Like paint, batteries, and other hazardous household items, do NOT throw CFLs in your household garbage. RECYCLE them safely at your local home improvement stores or check with your local waste management agency for recycling options and disposal guidelines in your community.

Tools/Supplies Needed:

Step Stool or Ladder

Screwdriver Hammer

Solar Powered Motion Sensor Floodlight   and/or

Solar Powered Accent/Path Lights

Approximate Time:

30 Minutes on Day #1 and Day #4

Now What?

For Motion Sensor Floodlights:

1. Remove light(s) from boxes and place solar device in a bright sunny place for at least 3 days, to charge the battery.
2. On Day Four, Install using screws provided. Place solar panel in the most sunny location that is within the reach of the cord connecting it to the light.
3. Mount the Light so the sensing device picks up from the angle of entry. Adjust the light to shine on the desired area of your walkway, driveway, home, etc. That's It!

For Accent/Path Lights:

1. Push light stakes into the ground, stake like. Unless the lights have a separate solar absorption panel, they will likely need to be exposed to some sunlight daily.
2. Follow simple instructions for re-charging batteries, if you experience many days of no sun (like winter in New England or Seattle).

Follow Factory Installation Instructions as there are many varieties of this style of lights.

NOTE: Whenever possible, I prefer the solar collector to be separate from the light(s). Makes it easier to charge the battery, when necessary.

Tools/Supplies Needed:
Phillips-head Screwdriver
Pencil
Proper Batteries (2) — if necessary
Programmable Thermostat

Time Needed:
About 45 minutes

Now What?

**READ AND FOLLOW ALL FACTORY ENCLOSED INSTRUCTIONS!
INSTRUCTIONS BELOW ARE FOR GENERAL GUIDANCE ONLY!**

1. Turn off breaker(s) for Heat and Air Conditioning System.
2. Remove OLD thermostat. Disconnect color-coded wires, keeping them separated.
   IMPORTANT: do not let bare wires touch each other!
3. Wrap wires around the pencil to keep them separate. Apply coding tags per directions.
4. Attach the back panel or mount for programmable thermostat with screws and/or wall anchors provided in the package.
5. Reconnect all wires, matching the codes and ***following the written factory instructions included*** with your thermostat.
6. Add batteries (if necessary) and snap on front.
7. Program according to directions.
8. If you have more than one unit, connect other thermostats in the same way.

Note: Program your thermostat to adjust according to your weekly work and/or travel schedule. Set on 85 degrees in summer and 45 degrees in winter (when you are gone), so things won't burn or freeze.

ALWAYS – Read enclosed factory instructions! Each make of thermostat is different and will install differently. Below is a ROUGH template on installation. Your instruction sheet will be SPECIFIC to your thermostat...so use YOUR instruction sheet.

1) TURN OFF ALL POWER & REMOVE OLD THERMOSTAT

2) MOUNT NEW THERMOSTAT & ATTACH WIRES TO SCREWS

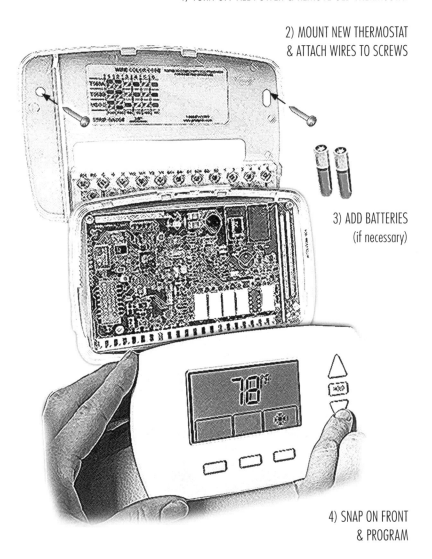

3) ADD BATTERIES
(if necessary)

4) SNAP ON FRONT & PROGRAM

Tools/Supplies Needed:

1 to 3 Power Strips with single shut off button
1 to 3 Light Timers (if desired)

Time Needed:

25 minutes

Now What?

Locate places in your home where multiple, power-draining gadgets remain **ON** all the time. A Kitchen is a real good place to start: try coffee makers, microwaves, appliances, and so on. Anything that has a light that stays on when you're not using it is consistently sucking energy, 24/7.

Take a power strip and plug in all the devices. When you go to bed and/or leave, turn it ALL off with a single flip of the switch. Plus, you'll free up some outlets!

Repeat this process with Living Room devices (stereos, televisions, DVD players) and Office devices (leaving a laser printer on all the time can raise your electric bill by several dollars each month!). You may need one in Bedrooms, too, so all electronic devices can be completely turned off when not in use.

As a rule, no single "energy vampire" uses that much electricity. But look at how many lights you still see when the house is otherwise dark ... COLLECTIVELY, it adds up!

OPTION: If you don't think you'll consistently remember to turn the power strips off before leaving, consider connecting them to a TIMER that's programmed according to your schedule – plug timer into wall and skip the worry!

Persons more knowledgeable than I have said it: "Water is the gold of the 21st Century".

Consider this: depending on which report you read, approximately $1/3^{rd}$ of the world's population has no access to CLEAN water! That is over 2 BILLION people drinking horribly polluted water. Millions get sick and/or die everyday from drinking water they must have to even live. $aving water is necessary for all of us to live...here on this very small planet.

If you doubt the drought and pollution shortages, take a look at your water bill (if you live in a dry climate; Austin, Phoenix or Albuquerque – to name a few). Now, look at the trend in stock prices of water related companies.

Observe that seven companies OWN the rights to much of the world's clean water supply. THINK about the implications of that one!

Water sustains all life on this planet; from the fish we eat to the cars and computers we build, water is at the base of it all. Even our bodies are more than half water! Each day there is less clean drinking water available. Increasing levels of chemicals, additives and purifiers are required to maintain minimal drinking standards.

Consider the EXPLOSION in bottled water businesses: 15 years ago, few of us would have "wasted our money" buying bottled water. Now, it is sold in almost every store in North America. Bottled water creates billions of pounds of plastic trash, which should be recycled but mostly is not. It takes hundreds of years for ONE plastic bottle to break down in a landfill.

Now Consider: if each person in the USA saves one cup of water per day we collectively save 50,000,000 GALLONS per day. This adds up to 18 BILLION GALLONS of water SAVED per year! ONE Cup Each. We can do that, at the very least!

EIGHTEEN. BILLION. Gallons.

These next easy projects will help you reduce your water consumption (and quite possibly your bill) and assist in making water cleaner and more available for a longer period in history – your grandkids will thank you ...

Tear out this list. Save for future trips, if you choose to buy these items on an "as needed" basis. This list does NOT include products from your General Shopping List.

Less Water ~ Great Flow! Project

Aerators reduce water CONSUMPTION while increasing water PRESSURE. I ORDER mine to get the reduction & great pressure I prefer. My aerators for bath sinks use .375 gallons per minute (gpm) in a spray. Kitchen sinks are .75 gpm in a single stream. Showers 1.75 gpm and the pressure is amazing. Home store prices are lower — but flow and/or pressure will be different. Go with what works best for you.

1 Faucet Aerator per bathroom sink @ $3-$15 ea _____

1 Showerhead Aerator per shower @ $30-$90 ea _____

Local Home/Hardware Store:

One small Pipe Wrench @ $5 _____

One roll of Teflon Pipe Tape @ $1 _____

Bottle It ~ Clean Water Project

Buy a Water Filtering System from $50 to $2500. Check the frequency and cost of filters and what pollutants are actually removed. From a counter-top Pitcher model @ $35 to a Reverse Osmosis System for under your sink @ $150 to a whole-house system @ $2500+.

Buy ONE _____

3- Stainless Steel Water Bottles per person @ $5-$9 ea _____

About Those Toilets! Project

ChemFree™ ToiletClean® Cartridge — one for EACH toilet $5 per toilet/sold in double packs at your local Home or Hardware store: _____

Stop It Up! ~ The Sink Stopper Project

Rubber Stoppers for all your sinks where your current stoppers do not work @ $1-$2 ea _____

STAPLE YOUR RECEIPTS HERE ON THIS PAGE!

Tools/Supplies Needed:

Shower Aerators under 1.75 gallons per minute (gpm) or less.

Sink Faucet Aerators—under .75 gpm for bath and 1 gpm for kitchen

Small Pipe Wrench

Rubber Jar Opener (for tightening)

A roll of Teflon Tape for pipe threads

Approximate Time:

1 Hour—Total

Now What?

1. Unscrew shower head and/or faucet head – dry it off. You may need to use your pipe wrench if they are on really tight.
2. Screw on flow reducers/aerators for faucets and the one for your shower; or install an actual Shower Aerator head. Hand tighten only!
3. Re-attach shower head – again, hand tighten only!
4. Turn on faucet and showerhead. No leaks? You are all set. Leaking? Tighten a bit more. Still leaking? Then...
5. Remove aerator, wrap end of faucet with 4"-6" of Teflon tape. Screw aerator on snugly. That should fix the leak.
6. Proceed to next faucet head and repeat until all are done.
7. Test for leaks by turning on ALL faucets and showers, one at a time. If they leak or spew, tighten them up some more. (Get "Mr. Muscles" next door to help you, if necessary)

Benefits

a. You will use MUCH LESS water and still have great PRESSURE and plenty of water for your tasks.

b. Bricor's reducers cut sink and shower flows dramatically with EXCELLENT pressure; this is why I am willing to pay more for them – and why they are mentioned here.

Quite Simply: Buy a Water Filtering System and buy 3 Stainless Steel Water Bottles per person in your home.

You can spend from $50 to $2500! There are a lot of good ones. Investigate the frequency and cost of filters. From counter-top models to a Reverse Osmosis System that goes under your sink, to a whole-house system — choose what works best for you and your budget.

MOST IMPORTANT!
Evaluate exactly WHAT the filters remove from your water. That is the critical issue!

My personal choices: a Reverse Osmosis System that installed under my kitchen sink with its own faucet. Cost today is about $100-$250.00 I am now in a much smaller space and use the pitcher style with 2 filters that need replacing about every 6 months.

Hints:

Any water filtering system in the $25-$250 range will generally pay for itself in a year or less..I drink 1-2 gallons of water per day x 365 days per year. That's 365 to 730 gallons of water per year for only ME! You may not drink that much, but imagine how much a family of four could save!

Consider:

If I spent only $.50 per gallon for bottled water, I would spend $182.50 to $365.00 for bottled water in 1 year. Most folks spend $1.50 for 16-20 oz.; that is a minimum of $4.50 per GALLON! More than a gallon of gasoline! Sip on that for a while!

Consider the additional trash bottled water creates, and all the resources and energy it takes to make those plastic bottles … and all the gas it takes to transport water all over the earth. How much sense does that make???

$ave Money … $ave your earth … $ave and preserve your good health!

Drink LOTS of Great Water!

I had water with a lot of minerals. As a result, I had to change my internal "toilet parts" more often because the minerals clog them, AND I had to really scrub to remove the calcium, lime and other minerals in the bowl as well as for cleanliness reasons!

The chemicals that it takes to remove the mineral deposits are generally noxious and toxic. Then we flush it into our water supply! Oh, Yummm....just what I want to drink!

Tools/Supplies Needed:

Your Two Hands
ChemFree™ ToiletClean® Cartridge – one for EACH toilet

Approximate Time Needed:

30 minutes total

Now What?

1. SCRUB your toilets and remove all minerals, stains and "gunk"...sorry, but you have to start with a clean toilet!
2. Remove ToiletClean® from packaging (re-cycle) and drop it inside your toilet's tank. That's it for 5-10 Years!
3. Repeat with additional toilets in your home!
4. Feeling generous? Do your kid's and parent's homes too!
5. Yes – yes! You will still have to clean your human waste from the toilet...common sense folks!

ToiletClean® does not contain harmful chemicals, and will not discolor your water! (Bye-bye blue or green or whatever!)

How many of your sink or tub drains work? Test them — run some water and see if it stays in the sink/tub. If all drains work, skip this one. If one or more fail to hold water measure the size of the drain hole and write it down.

Tools/Supplies Needed:
One Rubber Drain Stopper for each non-working sink
(come in various sizes) @ $.85-$1.50 each

Time Needed:
about 5-15 minutes per sink

Now What?
1. For sinks/tubs with NO up and down stopper, unwrap the new rubber stopper that fits and place on side of sink or tub so you'll remember to use it!
2. For sinks with non-working up and down plunger stopper, remove it. Stick your head under the sink — you will see where the stopper is hooked to the "up and down" pull handle above — a thin metal piece with holes in it.
3. If it is UNHOOKED than reconnect it and see if it operates properly, by repeating the "Test" above.
4. If it still does not work and/or there is no way to hook it than unhook it from that handle under the sink and remove it from sink, entirely.
5. Unwrap your new right-size sink stopper and place on side of sink (so you'll remember to use it!)

When you wash your face, feet or a few dirty dishes (depends on the sink!), insert the stopper, fill sink half full of warm water ... do the task and drain.

This saves THOUSANDS of gallons of water per year from flowing down the drain, compared to just turning the spigot on and leaving it running throughout the task.

Easy, huh?

Cheap, too!

Laundry and/or Dishwasher

1. Wash only FULL loads whenever possible.
2. Reduce water level for smaller loads of clothes.
3. Use COLD water. This saves energy and helps prevent clothes from shrinking and fading.
4. Buy an energy efficient Washer and Dryer when it is time for another one! Better yet, use a "Solar Dryer" — known as a clothes line!

Personal Hygiene Activities

1. Turn the sink water OFF or SLOW the FLOW when brushing teeth, rinsing dishes, washing hands or face.
2. Take shorter showers ~ a Fun Timer works great for those eternal "teenager" bath encounters!
3. Take showers instead of baths. Showers use about 1/3rd of the water a bath consumes!
4. Shower/Bathe every other day! UNLESS you are engaged in sweaty physical activity. C'mon ... try it for a month! I promise that I will not tell your mother! Side benefit — your adult SKIN will be better hydrated.

Outdoor Uses

1. Buy a DRIP Irrigation hose, available about anywhere for roughly $10. Wind it through your plants, pour mulch on top, hook it up and turn it on about half way in the evening, three times a week to water your plants directly. Saves loads of water and money.
2. If you water your grass:

    a) Consider removing it and replacing with native plants that don't require a lot of water to grow well in your area — this is called Xeri-Scaping. (Less work too!)

    b) When you mow, do so on the highest or next to highest level possible...leave it longer. Longer grass requires far less watering and will stay healthier and greener.
3. Get a couple of Rain barrels and collect water from your roof to water plants outdoors. Just Google 'Rain Water Harvesting' and/or 'Rain Water Collection' for more info.

Energy Saving Tip

Turn OFF your water heater at the breaker box before you leave home for the day and/or go to bed at night. Better yet, get a Water Heater TIMER. This will assist in reducing your electric bill by $10-$25 per month.

Have you experienced a fire in your home? Know of someone who has experienced a fire in their home?

Two of my friends lost everything in devestating fires. One lost her house and all its contents. The other spent thousands of dollars, having her home repaired . . . and most of her stuff cleaned or replaced.

How many of us have experienced (or know someone who has experienced) a burglary , or attempted burglary?

I experienced several attempted burglaries . . . they finally made it in one late afternoon while I was gone. This resulted in a major insurance claim and higher insurance rates for 5 years. They literally came in through the bathroom window.

These experiences are frightening, unnerving, scary. They change the way we see our security and our homes . . . AND they are largely preventable.

This segment provides long term solutions to help prevent fire and burglary. Again, the projects are easy and inexpensive. In many cases, they will help reduce your insurance rates; and they may just Save Your Life . . . or the life of your children, your spouse or your friends.

So, let's get started!

Tear out this list. Save for future trips, if you choose to buy these items on an "as needed" basis. This list does NOT include products from the General Shopping List.

$TOP $MOKING! $moke Detectors *Project*

3-7 Smoke Detectors (depending on size of house)
$5–$10 each – Total: $15–$70   _ _ _ _ _

$top $moking ~ Part II: Fire Extinguishers *Project*

2-5 "Home" Style Fire Extinguishers @ $10 each, to put out
fires in various areas of your home:
1 for KITCHEN/Grease Fires   _ _ _ _ _
1 for Each fireplace in the house   _ _ _ _ _
1 for every 2 bedrooms, with easy access   _ _ _ _ _
1 each for Garage, Basement & Attic   _ _ _ _ _

Lock It Down! *Project*

1 Deadbolt Lock per outside doors @ $15 ea   _ _ _ _ _
(Choose locking from inside only with no outside)
Drill – borrow one or buy one for $35-$90   _ _ _ _ _
Hole Saw for your drill or borrow one $10   _ _ _ _ _

Lock It Open! *Project*

Window "Thumb" Screw Locks
2 per window @ $2.50-$5.00 per set   _ _ _ _ _

Protecting Your Pipes *Project*

Foam Style, Slip-On, Self Adhesive Pipe Insulation
@ $5-$25 depends on length needed   _ _ _ _ _
Faucet Covers ($2-$5) for each outside faucet _ _ _ _ _

STAPLE YOUR RECEIPTS HERE ON THIS PAGE!

Tools/Supplies Needed:
Step Stool

3-7 Smoke Detectors (depending on size of house)

SHOULD include batteries!

Small Phillips-head Screwdriver – in your "toolbox"

Pencil (sharpened)

Time Needed:
30 minutes per detector

Now What?
1. Take step stool and pencil; begin close to or in Kitchen. Decide on location (ceiling or wall) for Smoke Detectors. Mark the spot with an "X"
2. Mark location for Smoke Detectors, in bedroom hallways. If all bedrooms are off one hall, locate detector half way down hall. Smoke Detectors should be on EACH floor of your home, including: BASEMENT – ATTIC – GARAGE
3. Grab screwdriver and smoke detectors. Screw mounting piece in each "X'd" location.
4. Insert battery (usually 9 volt) and close cover.
5. Slip and turn cover over mounting bracket per instructions!
6. Test "Beep" them to make sure they are working.
9. Rest easier.
10. **Test batteries every 3 months.** Add it to your calendar checklist – they can save your life – and your home!

Tools/Supplies Needed:

2-5 "Home" Style Fire Extinguishers

1 for KITCHEN/Grease Fires

1 for Each fireplace in the Home

1 for every 2 bedrooms or Main Hallway

1 each for Garage, Basement & Attic

Time Needed:

1 Hour of FAMILY Time

Now What?

1. Sit down with everyone in your home. READ and REVIEW instructions for the Kitchen Fire Extinguisher. Then place it within easy reach of the stove (like under the kitchen sink or in a cupboard in the "island" or pantry)

2. Meet in Living Room! Read instructions for putting out fireplace fires, if you have one! Place extinguisher(s) within easy reach of fireplace and where it will not be exposed to the fire and heat.

3. Meet in Bathroom. Read info on General Fires and related extinguishers. Place one Extinguisher in each bathroom or in any other general, easy to reach, centrally located place in your home.

4. Finally: Discuss, outline and implement an Emergency Home Evacuation Plan. Make sure everyone understands the Plan and how to escape in the event of a fire; including Calling 911 first, if possible!

5. Practice Evacuation plan weekly for a month. Monthly for 3 months. Quarterly for 3 years. Then annually for the rest of your life.

IT'S BEEN SAID BEFORE, BUT IT IS SO TRUE:
"THE LIFE YOU SAVE MAY BE YOUR OWN or
SOMEONE YOU LOVE."

Tools/Supplies Needed:

Deadbolt Locks for Outside Doors —Choose locking from
inside only with no outside lock or locking from both
inside and outside
Hole Saw and Drill — Borrow or Buy

Time Needed:

30—45 minutes per door

Now What?

1. Take everything out of the package (re-cycle packaging).
2. Read & follow the factory instructions for installation.
3. Place Hole Saw on drill according to instructions.
4. Draw hole template positions, as instructed, on the door.
5. Cut holes properly & install locks according to instructions.
6. If locks unlock from the outside, place key on key ring.
7. Instruct and illustrate to all family members on how to use the lock(s) and key(s).
8. If you are installing more than one lock, buy a double pack of deadbolts so they are keyed the same. This eliminates confusion on which key belongs to what lock.

Benefits:

a. A more secure, less "thief friendly" home.
b. Check to see if this may help you qualify for lower home owner insurance rates.

Tools/Supplies Needed:

Window "Thumb" Screw Locks – 2 per window

Also known as "mini-clamps" for windows!

Time Needed:

5 minutes per window

Now What?

1. Remove locks from packaging – recycle packaging
2. Place one (1) thumb screw lock on each side of your window frame, a few inches above the closed position.
3. You can adjust these easily. Ex: During delightful weather raise your windows 3" – 5". Place locks at the top of the adjustable window and screw the thumbscrews firmly into the frame.
4. Leave window open and enjoy the fresh air.

Benefits:

a. Fresh Air in your home is generally healthier for all.
b. Protection for your home
c. Reduced utility/energy bills by using fresh instead of "conditioned" air.

Smoke Detector attaches to wall or ceiling with screws.

Snap on cover. Don't forget to add batteries!

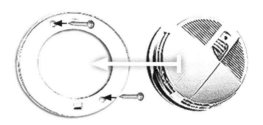

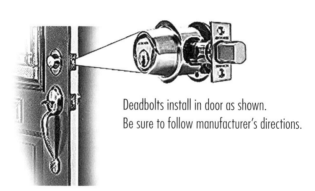

Deadbolts install in door as shown.
Be sure to follow manufacturer's directions.

Thumbscrew locks attach
to side of window.

Lock prevents window
from being raised.

Pipes? Huh? We're talking WATER pipes – and we're protecting your pipes from FREEZING up in the winter! Frozen pipes result in a PILE of damage to your home and possibly your neighbors', if you live in a condo, apartment or duplex. It is in everyone's best interest to keep pipes FROM freezing.

Common Sense Solution:

When temperatures drop below freezing for day, open the doors under your sinks to keep pipes warm; drip water from your faucets to prevent freezing. But there are other things you can do to help keep your pipes safe:

Tools/Supplies Needed:

Measuring Tape
Foam Style, Slip-On, Self Adhesive Pipe Insulation
Faucet Covers for each outside faucet

Time Needed:

30 minutes to 1 hour

Now What?

1. Measure the length AND diameter of ALL pipes exposed to extreme cold in the winter time. Check attic, basements, crawl space under the house, indoor plumbing close to outdoor walls and outdoor exposed pipes.
2. Write down the measurements; take them to your home improvement store and buy correct amount of insulation. It is generally slit on one side for slip-on installation.
4. Once home, remove packaging. Slide insulation over the exposed pipes and seal. Cut with a knife or scissors to achieve the correct lengths for complete pipe coverage.
5. Take faucet covers and place over outside faucets: latch hook onto spigot and tighten.

That's it folks!

Are you one of the millions of folks afflicted with allergies? As our outdoor, office and home environments become increasingly polluted and our ozone layer continues to disappear, challenges with allergies have risen dramatically in the last 20 years.

There are common sense choices we can all make:
1. Ride Share – fewer cars = less pollution
2. Use bicycles, public transportation or walk when practical. Check out New SCOOTERS, small motorcycles, motorized bicycles and tricycles. So many more great choices!
3. "Batch" your errands geographically. You'll drive less, accomplish more and save time and money.
4. Choose to buy Hybrid or Electric cars. The most readily available are Toyota Prius and Camry. Honda Civic, Insight and Accord. Ford Escape. The Leaf. The Volt. Smart Cars. The list goes on; our choices have never been better.

What about air quality INSIDE your home? What does it take to keep your air cleaner,healthier, circulating to maximize the heat or cold – depending on seasons?

CLEAN your ductwork and vents every two years. This may not be possible if you have "flex ducts" – ask your HVAC specialist. Clean the exterior "vent covers" thoroughly every year. Mine are metal and go in my dishwasher twice a year!

Now here are a few more projects to help you and yours breathe easier:

Tear out this list. Save for future trips, if you choose to buy these items on an "as needed" basis. This list does NOT include products from your General Shopping List.

Circulating Comfort! Project

Ceiling Fan, Sized for Your Room @ $55-$250 _____

Heavy Duty Razor Knife @ $2-$5 _____

Expandable Ceiling Fan Hanger Bar @ $15 (maybe) _____

Check with Store Person on whether you need this...

Heavy Duty Ceiling Fan Fixture Box @ $3 _____

Check with Store Person on whether you need this...

Fans OVER 35 lbs. need a "J" Hook — ask your store helper!

Cleaning Your Home's Air — Project

6 Pleated Air Filters @ $4-$20 each _____

(My filters generally last 3 months.)

STAPLE YOUR RECEIPTS HERE ON THIS PAGE!

Tools/Supplies Needed:

Ruler or Tape Measure
Screw Drivers – Phillips and Straight
Ceiling Fan(s)–Right Sized for Rooms
Short Ladder or Step Stool
Expandable Ceiling Fan Hanger Bar

Flashlight
Pencil
"J" Hook
Heavy Duty Razor Knife
Heavy Duty Ceiling Fan Fixture Box

Time Needed:

1 hour per Fan

HINT! Take a Ceiling Fan installation "class" from your home improvement store. It helps!

Now What?

1. Decide fan location. It is easiest to replace a light fixture and use existing wiring. Mark the spot. Unpack fan. *READ & FOLLOW Manufacturer's Installation Instructions!*

2. TURN OFF THE POWER to that location; remove fixture & box OR cut a 4" circle from ceiling sheet rock where fan is to be placed. Peer into ceiling; are there board supports?

3. Locate the nearest electrical wires or existing wires.

4. Find the 2 closest side-by-side ceiling joists. Slip Hanger Bar through the hole and extend until it grasps each board.

5. Attach fan box to the support bar. If using a former fixture location, remove lightweight box and replace with heavy duty box. Attach it SECURELY!

6. Pull wires through the round mounting plate and screw plate into the fan box above it.

7. Thread the wires through the down rod. (Fan should hang down at least 6" with blades @ 1' from ceiling for best operation).

8. Following the factory's "Instruction Sheet" wire fan. Use Wire Nuts to secure wiring connections. Join bare grounding wires/ green wires. If there are lights, match white wires with each other & black wires with each other.

9. Assemble fan. Attach canopy (see fan installation instructions) into ceiling plate.

10. If fan has a light fixture, pull the wires through the light switch housing and attach light fixture to fan.

11. Install vibration-resistent compact fluorescent light bulbs.

12. Turn power on. Test fan and lights to make sure they work. Fan goes clockwise in the summer and counter clockwise in the winter. Enjoy feeling more comfortable.

Tools/Supplies Needed:

Tape Measure
6 Pleated Paper Air Filters

Time Needed:

10 Minutes

Now What?

1. Find the Return Air Vent in your home. This is where the air is sucked into the vent (as opposed to being blown out). It is quite large and hard to miss.
2. Find your air filter and NOTE the size. Write this down.
3. Buy Pleated Paper Air Filters at the size noted. For odd sizes — say 12" x 30" — simply fold a 12" x 36" filter 6" in and install. MOST filters are a standard size!
4. Remove any covering (like plastic bag) from filter — recycle in the plastic bag recycling bin at your local grocery.
5. Remove old filter (it will probably be dark colored & "gunky" looking). Install fresh filter. That gunky stuff was filtered from the air in your home!
6. Store spare air filters in a convenient location. Mark your calendar or the front of your return air vent for 2-3 months later; that is when you will need to change it again.
   OR
   Some of these filter companies will send you an on-line reminder if you sign up for it! How convenient is that?

NOTE:

During heavy use months of summer or winter, CHANGE the filter every TWO (2) months! If you have pets, you may have to change more often.

BENEFITS:

Pleated filters remove more "stuff" from your air and let your HVAC system work more efficiently. This makes for cleaner air, and possibly, a less dusty home and lower utility bills. For sure, it will help preserve and lengthen the life of your HVAC system!

Congratulations! You made it! Trusting, of course, you completed ALL of these little projects, applicable to your home, you now have extra money from utility bill savings each month.

More importantly, you are making a positive difference in supporting life on this planet. By using less — and $aving more — all humans, plants, and animals have a better chance being here for the next seven generations. Think about your Kids, Grandkids, Great-Grandkids!

Many people think "Environmental Conservation" is time-consuming, impractical, irrelevant or expensive ... and that "using less" means "being deprived." After completing the projects in this book, does it feel like that to you *now?*

Your home is more comfortable and, far from being deprived, you now have more money in your pocket! (Of course, the utility companies are now deprived of YOUR hard earned money ... breaks your heart, doesn't it?)

Please, pass this information on to your family and friends ... ask the person, company or organization who gave you this book for another dozen! Or, check out the order information in the back of this book or our website at:

www.weatherizedhomesinitiative.com

Yes, there is more ... there is always more ... so for those of you who "want more", what follows are more freebies from me to you ... together we are making a better world.

Sustainability is a Journey
Not a Destination!

Write the PHONE NUMBER for Local Recycling Provider Here:

_____

Ask specifically what can be recycled and how that needs to be handled. Or check the outside of your recycle bin and/or monthly statement. Write specifics down here:

Plastics – What number plastics do they take?   _____

Glass – usually ALL glass can be recycled   _____

Paper – what kinds? Magazines?   _____

Cans – nearly ALL aluminum cans can be recycled   _____

Yard Waste – how is that handled? Bundled?   _____

Typically:

1. **Plastics** including: water/juice bottles, milk jugs, hard plastic packaging is recycled.
2. All **glass** can be recycled EXCEPT: broken windows, old porcelain fixtures, etc.
3. All **paper** can be recycled, including: newspapers, yellow pages, magazines and "white" office type paper. Check on cardboard boxes for your area.
4. All **Cans** – both aluminum and steel.
5. **Yard Waste** is often placed in brown YARD WASTE bags and recycled into good dirt. Why not start your own COMPOST pile and recycle your own yard waste and food garbage and keep your own good dirt?

Organize It:

1. Rinse all gunk and goo from recyclables before recycling
2. Put paper in a paper sack, or tie newspapers with cotton twine, according to your AREA specifications and regulations. If you have Single Stream recycling, toss it in the bin!
3. PLASTIC BAGS and all sorts of plastic wrappings. Collect these and return to your GROCERY STORE. Most now have bins. Do NOT place in your recycling bin!!!

Please tell me you are bringing CLOTH/Rewoven/Recycled Totes when you shop!

IF there is no curbside recycling in your area, start to lobby for it! Or, place in appropriate sacks and take to your nearest recycling facility.

TecHnoLogical TraSH = eWaSte

What to do with old Technology:

Computers	Fax/Copy Machines		TVs/ VCRs/DVD Players	Cell Phones
Printers	Monitors	Keyboards	Batteries Stereos	Microwaves

Billions of pounds of technological waste – called "eWaste" – are dumped into landfills every year. This stuff NEVER degrades and POISONS our water, earth and air. What to do? Corporate America is starting to respond. The chart below is a very brief overview of companies who'll help you responsibly recycle or re-purpose tech gear. The list is by no means exhaustive, and company policies are subject to change. But some resources as of this writing include:

	BATTERIES	CFL BULBS	COMPUTERS	INK/TONER	MOBILE	TELEVISIONS	OTHER	FOR MORE INFO
Apple			Yes!		Yes!		iPods, also; Potential discount or gift card for working items.	www.apple.com/recycling
at&t					Yes!		Collects old phones and distributes them to soldiers with prepaid minutes.	www.wireless.att.com
Best Buy			Yes!	Yes!	Yes!	Yes!	Also has used appliance pick-up; fees may apply; not all stores offer all services.	www.bestbuy.com/recycling
Dell			Yes!	Yes!	Yes!		Items can be dropped off at Goodwill Stores; some locations take TVs, as well.	reconnectpartnership.com
(game)			Yes!		Yes!		Partners with Dell, Microsoft; also accept XBox, Zune, and accessories.	reconnectpartnership.com
Home Depot	Yes!	Yes!					Some stores only accept recyclables during special recycling drives.	www.homedepot.com/ecooptions
Lowe's	Yes!	Yes!			Yes!		Will haul away/recycle old appliances free with purchase of new appliance.	www.lowes.com
Office Depot			Yes!	Yes!	Yes!		Offers program rewards for recycling ink/toner cartridges; Fees apply for tech.	www.officedepot.cc/environment
Panasonic			Yes!	Yes!	Yes!	Yes!	Offers discount on new products with trade-in of qualifying computers.	www.panasonic.com/environmental
SHARP	Yes!		Yes!	Yes!	Yes!	Yes!	No charge for Sharp televisions; may be fees for other brands/products.	www.sharpusa.com
SONY			Yes!			Yes!	Up to medium size of any brand; any size Sony.	green.sel.sony.com
Sprint					Yes!		Offers customers credit on 100s of wireless devices; recycles others free.	www.sprint.com
STAPLES	Yes!		Yes!	Yes!	Yes!		Fees may apply; Technicians can download data from old devices to new ones.	www.staples.com
TARGET				Yes!	Yes!		Some items may qualify for rewards in the form of Target Gift Cards.	hereforgood.target.com
T-Mobile					Yes!		Recycles all brands/models of wireless phones, batteries, PDAs, and accessories.	www.t-mobile.com
TOSHIBA			Yes!	Yes!		Yes!	Partners w/ Cristina Foundation to provide tech to children with disabilities.	us.toshiba.com/green/reuse-and-recycling
verizon					Yes!		Donated phones are refurbished & given to domestic violence organizations.	www.verizonwireless.com

MORE RESOURCES: To find a responsible eWaste recycler near you: www.e-Stewards.org
Cell Phone recyclers/buy backs: www.capstonewirelessllc.com and www.call2recycle.org
Manufacture Take Back Programs: www.electonicstakeback.com
Non-working? Contact the manufacturer about recycling provisions, or www.goodwill.org

... sometimes costs more than the product!

In retail, packaging is "everything". Don't think so? Look at cereal boxes, computer games, liquid cleaning stuff and over-the-counter pills (to name a few)! Enticing! Over-packaged! Built for consumerism! Ya' gotta buy it ... **NOT!**

You CAN make a difference with your MONEY and OPINION! Here are a few simple ways:

1. Buy cereal and other staples in re-closeable bags or in bulk.
2. Buy LARGE containers of frequently used product and transfer to smaller containers instead of buying lots of smaller containers. (This usually ave money too). Stuff like sulfate, sodium laureth-free shampoo & conditioners, phosphate free, biodegradable laundry soap, fabric softner, NON-antibacterial hand soap, olive oil and organic yogurt.
3. Remove excess packaging from products AFTER you have paid for them. Take to the store manager and request they recycle it! If enough of us did this, especially in the "Big Box" stores ... the store would DEMAND that manufacturers reduce the packaging! (Some manufacturers are "seeing the light", and are already moving in this direction.)
4. SAVE food jars, plastic containers, plastic bags and re-use! Over and over and over. I have not purchased any storage containers or 'zipper' bags in years. Why? They are everywhere for FREE! So why buy? Just rinse or wash and re-use. I recycle many of these containers at the end of each calendar year and start over again.
5. BRING YOUR OWN BAG (BYOB!) when you shop. Kick the plastic habit. Ever hear of the Pacific Ocean garbage patch filled with plastic? Check out: www.greatgarbagepatch.org NOW! Make a different choice!

Why is cotton in a lot of pill bottles? Why do they put secure bottles in colorful boxes? Why put a $20 memory chip in a huge plastic package? Why are "cleaning products" (most of which are POISONOUS) that are mostly water put in large containers, when the essential ingredients could be sold in pouches (like some dishwasher soaps) and we could add water ourselves! Think about the GAS $aved trucking it across country! Why isn't ALL toilet paper made from recycled paper? Why do we insist on wiping our behinds with freshly cut trees?

Vote with your $$$, folks! CALL those toll-free numbers and be HEARD and SAVE money!

We all have a voice. Use it or lose it!

This is it: the last little "goodies" from me to you for now.

You're saving money on your utility bills, feeling good about throwing out less trash, because you are recycling your paper, cans, plastic, glass, etc. You no longer buy bottled water and you are spending less for stuff with too much packaging by choosing products with less packaging. **Be PROUD of YOU!**

Here's the kicker: in order to make recycled stuff profitable we must BUY products made from stuff that is recycled! I mean, we can recycle all the stuff in the universe, but if we don't CHOOSE to buy things made from recycled stuff, what is the point?

So: what can be bought — EASILY — that is recycled, attractive, and useful? Here are a few everyday things. Bring your *reusable shopping tote bags* and choose. . . .

Toilet Paper, Trash Sacks, Napkins, Paper Plates, Paper Cups, and Paper Towels, Compostable 'plastic' knives-forks-spoons made from recycled paper and plastic.

Best places to find them: COSTCO. HEB. CENTRAL MARKET (grocery stores in TX). WHOLE FOODS. TRADER JOES. OFFICE DEPOT. I do not like shopping (the Shopping Gene missed me!), so there are probably more places that now stock these items. LOOK for them. ASK your local Wal-Mart and Target . . . after all they have signs in their stores that say "Reduce — Reuse — Recycle", so let's take 'em up on that!

Copy/Printer Paper, Large Brown Envelopes, File Folders, Corn Starch Packing Peanuts, PENS (from recycled plastic), 3-Ring Binders (from recycled paper) are in Office Supply stores already. OFFICE DEPOT and STAPLES have a good selection, the others may too. ASK!

Trash Cans, Rulers, Piggy Banks, Key Chains, Dog/Cat Food & Water Dishes, Pails, Picture Frames, Magnets, Tote Bags, Color Books, Funnels. Again, you must ASK for it: without "Demand" there is no "Supply"! Remember, the Good Book says: "Ask and ye shall receive" — it says nothing about, "hope and you will get!" Got it?

Calendars, Day Planners, Desk Pad Calendars, Books, Notepads, Pencils, Pens. First stop should be Office Depot or Staple. If what you want is not in your office supply store, "ASK and ye shall receive! "

Greeting Cards: Available almost everywhere now.

Carpet & Floor Coverings: Huh? Carpet? Yes, made from recycled pop bottles or from recycled carpet itself; floor coverings from cork, bamboo, etc. Feels GREAT, lasts a LONG time, is stain resistant. Most carpet companies make recycled/recyclable floor coverings; if you are going to install carpet, request it. Local carpet stores either carry it or can easily get it for you.

Plastic Cups, Frisbees, Pens, Bookmarks, Color books, Awards, All types of promotional items.   With our without your logo. Made from recycled and/or corn plastics. Ask your promotional products specialist.

Decking for your Home. Trex and Choice Deck (the two brands with which I am familiar) are both made from recycled wood products, saw dust and plastics. Best of all, they require NO staining (unless you just want to) and will NEVER rot, buckle, warp or need to be sealed. They're truly NO/ LOW maintenance Life Time Decks. It may cost a bit more to put them in, but you'll make that back in the first 3-5 years from no maintenance...AND they'll NEVER put a splinter in anyone's foot!

Buy Products Packaged in Recycled Stuff
Like crackers! Check out the cracker boxes (when not available in bags) some factories make their boxes from recycled paper. Aveda hair product bottles are made from recycled plastic. Start reading those labels. Look for the little "arrow triangles" to see if the packaging or product can be recycled or if it is made from recycled stuff.

A Word of "Advice"
For heaven's sake, quit consuming BLEACH — it is TOXIC! Buy UNBLEACHED flour, sugar and coffee filters. Borax and hydrogen peroxide will produce WHITE laundry too!

As you do these projects, you will discover or invent other inexpensive energy saving Home Improvements. So, we're having a little contest ...

Complete all these projects, relevant to need ... make a copy of your receipts ... and mail them in with your suggested Easy Home Improvement that saves or improves your homes:
> Air   Water   Utilities   Earth

If we select your idea for publication and you agree to let us use it, you'll receive your choice of a new Reverse Osmosis Water Filtration System (under the sink model) or a $250.00 Sustainable Flooring Coupon! AND your name will be credited in our next book!

The Rules:
> Project must cost LESS than $100.
> It must be a project and not a behavior change.
> Most people should be able to do it.

If 2 or more similar improvements are selected, the one received first will be awarded.

Email from our website: ***www.weatherizedhomesinitiative.com***
www.bestgreenhomeprojects.com
www.eco-uno.com

Snail-mail to: 20/20 Enterprises, Inc.
                   Home Improvement Dept.
                   3005 S Lamar Blvd, D109-289
                   Austin, TX 78704

Friend us on Facebook! Follow us on Twitter. And Contribute to our Blog!

Thanks to all of you. Happy Projecting!